Culture Around the World

by Jody Jackson

PEARSON

Glenview, Illinois • Boston, Massachusetts • Mesa, Arizona
Shoreview, Minnesota • Upper Saddle River, New Jersey

The United States has many cultures.

Culture is the way people live their lives. The foods people eat are part of their culture. So are language, music, and holidays. Every place in the world has a culture. The United States has people from all over the world. It has many different cultures.

pizza

Pizza comes from Italy.

Do you like nibbling pizza? Did you know pizza comes from Italy? Many foods and their names come from other countries.

Do you like to eat hamburgers? The word *hamburger* means "from Hamburg, Germany." What other foods names do you know that come from other cultures?

Families light candles for Kwanzaa.

Children wear red clothes for Lunar New Year.

Holidays

People from different cultures celebrate different holidays. Kwanzaa is a holiday for some African Americans.

The New Year is a big holiday in China. It comes about a month after our New Year. What is your favorite holiday?

In India people speak many languages.

Languages

What languages do you know? In Mexico, most people speak Spanish. In India, many people speak Hindi. But India has many other languages. Some Indians know three languages, including English.

Music

What kind of music do you like? Music can be very different from culture to culture. The music we listen to may sound different from the music of another culture. Sometimes musicians take sounds from two cultures to make a new kind of music.

Cultures Come Together

People come to the United States from all around the world. They bring different foods, holidays, music, and languages with them. Their cultures have become part of our American culture.

The United States is a great place to find different cultures. It is fun to try new foods. It is fun to learn new words and hear new music. What do you like the most about your culture?

Index

This index tells where to find different parts of culture that you read about in this book.